D0762268

The Cognitive Style of PowerPoint

"Not waving but drowning." Stevie Smith

IN corporate and government bureaucracies, the standard method for making a presentation is to talk about a list of points organized onto slides projected up on the wall. For many years, overhead projectors lit up transparencies, and slide projectors showed high-resolution 35mm slides. Now "slideware" computer programs for presentations are nearly everywhere. Early in the 21st century, several hundred million copies of Microsoft PowerPoint were turning out trillions of slides each year.

Alas, slideware often reduces the analytical quality of presentations. In particular, the popular PowerPoint templates (ready-made designs) usually weaken verbal and spatial reasoning, and almost always corrupt statistical analysis. What is the problem with PowerPoint? And how can we improve our presentations?

When Louis Gerstner became president of IBM, he encountered a big company caught up in ritualistic slideware-style presentations:

> One of the first meetings I asked for was briefing on the state of the [mainframe computer] business. I remember at least two things about that first meeting with Nick Donofrio, who was then running the System/390 business. One is that I . . . experienced a repeat of my first day on the job. Once again, I found myself lacking a badge to open the doors at the complex, which housed the staffs of all of IBM's major product groups, and nobody there knew who I was. I finally persuaded a kind soul to let me in, found Nick, and we got started. Sort of.

> At that time, the standard format of any important IBM meeting was a presentation using overhead projectors and graphics that IBMers called "foils" [projected transparencies]. Nick was on his second foil when I stepped to the table and, as politely as I could in front of his team, switched off the projector. After a long moment of awkward silence, I simply said, "Let's just talk about your business."

> I mention this episode because it had an unintended, but terribly powerful ripple effect. By that afternoon an e-mail about my hitting the Off button on the overhead projector was crisscrossing the world. Talk about consternation! It was as if the President of the United States had banned the use of English at White House meetings.[1]

There is a lot going on here: the humiliation ceremony authorizing entry into the Corporate Palace, a new president symbolically demonstrating that things were going to be different from now on, and a blunt action indicating that there might be better ways to do serious analysis than reading aloud from projected lists—*"Let's just talk about your business."*

[1] Louis V. Gerstner, Jr., *Who Says Elephants Can't Dance? Inside IBM's Historic Turn-around* (2002), p. 43.

The Cognitive Style of PowerPoint

Gerstner's idea, *"Let's just talk about your business,"* means an exchange of information, an interplay between speaker and audience. Yet PowerPoint is entirely *presenter-oriented,* and *not content-oriented, not audience-oriented.* The claims of PP marketing are addressed to speakers: "A cure for the presentation jitters." "Get yourself organized." "Use the AutoContent Wizard to figure out what you want to say." The fans of PowerPoint are presenters, rarely audience members.

Slideware helps speakers to outline their talks, to retrieve and show diverse visual materials, and to communicate slides in talks, printed reports, and internet. And also to replace serious analysis with chartjunk, over-produced layouts, cheerleader logotypes and branding, and corny clip art. That is, PowerPointPhluff.

PP convenience for the speaker can be costly to both content and audience. These costs result from the *cognitive style characteristic of the standard default PP presentation:* foreshortening of evidence and thought, low spatial resolution, a deeply hierarchical single-path structure as the model for organizing every type of content, breaking up narrative and data into slides and minimal fragments, rapid temporal sequencing of thin information rather than focused spatial analysis, conspicuous decoration and Phluff, a preoccupation with format not content, an attitude of commercialism that turns everything into a sales pitch.

Extremely Low Resolution of PowerPoint

PP slides projected up on the wall are very low resolution—compared to paper, 35mm slides, and the immensely greater capacities of the human eye-brain system. Impoverished space leads to over-generalizations, imprecise statements, slogans, lightweight evidence, abrupt and thinly-argued claims. For example, this slide from a statistics course shows a seriously incomplete statement. Probably the *shortest true statement* that can be made about causality and correlation is *"Empirically observed covariation is a necessary but not sufficient condition for causality."* Or perhaps *"Correlation is not causation but it sure is a hint."* Many true statements are too long to fit on a PP slide, but this does not mean we should abbreviate the truth to make the words fit. It means we should find a better way to make presentations.

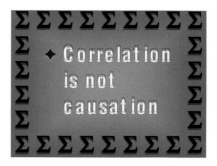

With so little information per slide, many many slides are needed. Audiences consequently endure a relentless sequentiality, one damn slide after another. When information is stacked in time, it is difficult to understand context and evaluate relationships. Visual reasoning usually works more effectively when the relevant information is shown adjacent in space within our eyespan. This is especially the case for statistical data, where the fundamental analytical act is to make comparisons.

The statistical graphics generated by the PowerPoint ready-made templates are astonishingly thin, nearly content-free. In 28 books on PP presentations, the 217 data graphics depict an average of 12 numbers each. Compared to the worldwide publications shown in the table at right, the statistical graphics based on PP templates are the thinnest of all, except for those in *Pravda* back in 1982, when that newspaper operated as the major propaganda instrument of the Soviet communist party and a totalitarian government. Doing a bit better than *Pravda* is not good enough. Data graphics based on PP templates show 10% to 20% of the information found in routine news graphics. The appropriate response to such vacuous displays is for people in the audience to speak out: *"It's more complicated than that!" "Why are we having this meeting? The rate of information transfer is asymptotically approaching zero."*

Bullet Outlines Dilute Thought

Impoverished resolution coerces slide-makers into using the compressed language of presentations—the *bullet list* of brief phrases. Bullets, little marks sometimes decorative or cute, signal the beginning of each phrase for those unable to recognize it. Sometimes the bullet hierarchies are so complex and intensely nested that they resemble computer code.

By insisting that points be placed in an orderly structure, the bullet list may help extremely disorganized speakers get themselves organized. The bullet list is surely the most widely used format in corporate and government presentations. Bullets show up in many paper reports, as presenters simply print out their PP slides.

For the naive, bullet lists may create the appearance of hard-headed organized thought. But in the reality of day-to-day practice, the PP cognitive style is faux-analytical. A study in the *Harvard Business Review* found generic, superficial, simplistic thinking in the bullet lists widely used in business planning and corporate strategy. What the authors are saying here, in the *Review's* earnestly diplomatic language, is that bullet outlines can make us stupid:

> In every company we know, planning follows the standard format of the bullet outline. . . [But] bullet lists encourage us to be lazy in three specific, and related ways.
>
> **Bullet lists are typically too generic.** They offer a series of things to do that could apply to any business. . . .
>
> **Bullets leave critical relationships unspecified.** Lists can communicate only three logical relationships: sequence (first to last in time); priority (least to most important or vice versa); or simple membership in a set (these items relate to one another in some way, but the nature of that relationship remains unstated). And a list can show only one of those relationships at a time.[2]

MEDIAN NUMBER OF ENTRIES IN DATA MATRICES FOR STATISTICAL GRAPHICS IN VARIOUS PUBLICATIONS, 2003	
Science	> 1,000
Nature	> 700
New York Times	120
Wall Street Journal	112
Frankfurter Allgemeine Zeitung	98
New England Journal of Medicine	53
The Lancet	46
Asahi	40
Financial Times	40
Time	37
The Economist	32
Le Monde	28
28 textbooks on PowerPoint presentations (1997-2003)	12
Pravda (1982)	5

Here is a graphic from *Pravda* (May 24, 1982), in the low-content, high-Phluff style now emulated by PP templates:

Рост продукции промышленности (1922 г. = 1).

Additional evidence on data matrices for various publications, including *Pravda*, is reported in Edward R. Tufte, *The Visual Display of Quantitative Information* (1983, 2001), p. 167. In this table above, the medians are based on at least 20 statistical graphics and at least one full issue of each publication. Except for scientific journals, most of these publications use standard formats issue after issue; replications of several of the counts above were within 10% of the original result.

[2] Gordon Shaw, Robert Brown, Philip Bromiley, "Strategic Stories: How 3M is Rewriting Business Planning," *Harvard Business Review*, 76 (May-June, 1998), pp. 42-44.

By leaving out the narrative between the points, the bullet outline ignores and conceals the causal assumptions and analytic structure of the reasoning. In their *Harvard Business Review* paper on business planning, Shaw, Brown, and Bromiley show that even simple one-way causal models are vague and unspecified in bullet outlines. And more realistic multivariate models with feedback loops and simultaneity are way over the head of the simplistic bullets:

Bullets leave critical assumptions about how the business works unstated. Consider these major objectives from a standard five-year strategic plan:

- Increase market share by 25%.
- Increase profits by 30%.
- Increase new-product introductions to ten a year.

Implicit in this plan is a complex but unexplained vision of the organization, the market, and the customer. However, we cannot extrapolate that vision from the bullet list. The plan does not tell us how these objectives tie together and, in fact, many radically different strategies could be represented by these three simple points. Does improved marketing increase market share, which results in increased profits (perhaps from economies of scale), thus providing funds for increased new-product development?

Market share ⟶ Profits ⟶ New-product development

Or maybe new-product development will result in both increased profits and market share at once:

New-product development ⟶ Market share
New-product development ⟶ Profits

Alternatively, perhaps windfall profits will let us just buy market share by stepping up advertising and new-product development:

Profits ⟶ New-product development ⟶ Market share[3]

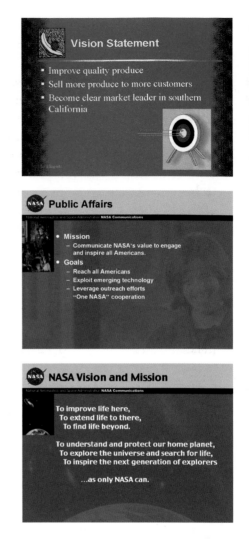

Bullet outlines might be useful in presentations now and then, but *sentences* with subjects and verbs are usually better. Instead of this type of soft, generic point found in many business plans

✓ *Accelerate the introduction of new products!*

it would be better to say *who* might do it and *how, when, and where* they might do it. Then several sentences together in a row, a *narrative,* could spell out the specific methods and processes by which the generic feel-good goals of mission statements might be achieved. Presentations for strategic planning might go beyond the words in lists and sentences by using annotated diagrams, images, sketches of causal models, equations, tables of numbers, and multivariate evidence.

[3] Gordon Shaw, Robert Brown, Philip Bromiley, "Strategic Stories: How 3M is Rewriting Business Planning," *Harvard Business Review*, 76 (May-June, 1998), p. 44. © 1998 Harvard Business School Publishing Corporation, all rights reserved.

As in corporate planning, bullet outlines are also far from the optimal format for scientific and engineering analysis. Indeed such outlines may well be pessimal.

Our evidence begins with a case study of 3 PowerPoint presentations directed to NASA officials who were making some important decisions during the final flight of the space shuttle Columbia. Those presentations contained several intellectual failures in engineering analysis. In addition, the cognitive style of PP compromised the analysis. Furthermore, the PP damage to these presentations turns out to reflect *widespread* problems in technical communication by means of PP, according to the final report of the Columbia Accident Investigation Board.

During the spaceflight of the shuttle Columbia in January 2003, Boeing Corporation engineers prepared 3 quick reports assessing possible damage to the left wing resulting from the impact of several chunks of debris 81 seconds after liftoff.[4] Although the evidence is uncertain and thin, the logical structure of the engineering analysis is straightforward:

debris *kinetic energy*
(function of mass,   +   debris hits locations
velocity, and angle   of *varying vulnerability*   ⟶   *level of threat* to the
of incidence)   on left wing   Columbia during
                                                                 re-entry heating
                                                                 of wing

The Columbia Accident Investigation Board found that the reports unfortunately provided an over-optimistic assessment of the danger facing the damaged Columbia as it orbited. All 3 reports have standard PP format problems: elaborate bullet outlines; segregation of words and numbers (12 of 14 slides with quantitative data have no accompanying analysis); atrocious typography; data imprisoned in tables by thick nets of spreadsheet grids; only 10 to 20 short lines of text per slide.

And now, on the next page, let us take a close look at the key slide in the Boeing PowerPoint reports on the Columbia.

[4] Carlos Ortiz, Arturo Green, Jack McClymonds, Jeff Stone, Abdi Khodadoust, "Preliminary Debris Transport Assessment of Debris Impacting Orbiter Lower Surface in STS-107 Mission," January 21, 2003; P. Parker, D. Chao, I. Norman, M. Dunham, "Orbiter Assessment of STS-107 ET Bipod Insulation Ramp Impact," January 23, 2003; Carlos Ortiz, "Debris Transport Assessment of Debris Impacting Orbiter Lower Surface in STS-107 Mission," January 24, 2003. The Boeing reports are published in official records of the Columbia investigation.

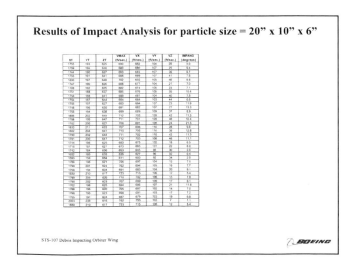

8

On this single Columbia slide, in a PowerPoint festival of bureaucratic hyper-rationalism, 6 different levels of hierarchy are used to classify, prioritize, and display 11 simple sentences:

Level 1   Title of Slide
Level 2   ● Very Big Bullet
Level 3   — dash
Level 4   ◆ diamond
Level 5   • little bullet
Level 6   ( ) parentheses ending level 5

The analysis begins with the dreaded "Executive Summary." A conclusion is presented as a headline title: "Test Data Indicates Conservatism for Tile Penetration." This turns out to be unmerited reassurance. Executives, at least those who don't want to get fooled, had better read far beyond the title.

The "conservatism" is *not* about the predicted tile damage but rather about the *choice of models* that might be used to predict damage! But why, after 112 flights, are models being calibrated during a crisis? How can "conservatism" be inferred from a loose comparison of a computer model and some thin data? Divergent evidence means divergent evidence, not inferential security. Claims of analytic "conservatism" should be viewed with skepticism. Such claims are sometimes a rhetorical tactic that substitutes verbal fudge factors for quantitative assessments.

As the analysis continues, the seemingly reassuring conclusion of the headline fades away.

These lower-level bullets at the end of the slide reveal that the headline conclusion is irrelevant and diverting. This third-level point notes that "Flight condition [that is, the Columbia] is significantly outside of test database." How far outside? The final bullet will tell us.

This fourth-level bullet concluding the slide says that, by the way, the debris that struck the Columbia is estimated to be $1920/3 = 640$ times larger than data used in the tests of the model! Thus a better headline would be "Review of Test Data Indicates Irrelevance of Two Models." There is an interesting dynamic to this slide: the headline is an exercise in misdirection, which the text then awkwardly and slowly eviscerates.

The Very-Big-Bullet sentence does not seem to make sense.

Spray On Foam Insulation

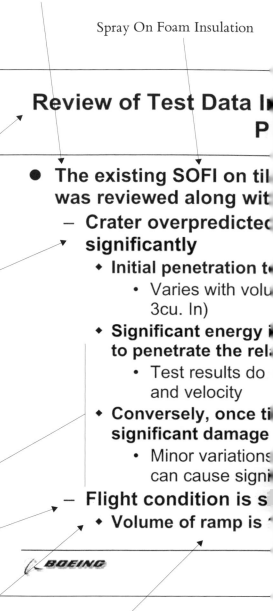

A reference to a foam insulation piece that separated from the bipod ramp tying the or to the large liquid fuel tank. Instead of "ra say "estimated volume of one of several p of debris that might have damaged the wi

A model to estimate damage to
the tiles protecting the left wing

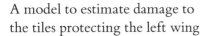

Conservatism for Tile
n

used to create Crater
outhwest Research data
on of tile coating

by normal velocity
projectile (e.g., 200ft/sec for

or the softer SOFI particle
tile coating
s possible at sufficient mass

ated SOFI can cause

rgy (above penetration level)
mage

outside of test database
s 3 cu in for test

6

n their final report (p. 191), the Columbia Accident
vestigation Board developed this point about units
measurement: "While such inconsistencies might
em minor, in highly technical fields like aerospace
gineering a misplaced decimal point or mistaken
it of measurement can easily engender inconsisten-
es and inaccuracies."

The vaguely quantitative words "significant" and
"significantly" are used 5 times on this slide, with *de facto*
meanings ranging from "detectable in largely irrelevant
calibration case study" to "an amount of damage so that
everyone dies" to "a difference of 640-fold." None of
these 5 usages appears to refer to the technical meaning
of "statistical significance."

The low resolution of PowerPoint slides promotes
the use of compressed phrases like "Tile Penetration."
As is the case here, such phrases may well be ambiguous.
The low resolution and large font generate 3 typographic
orphans, lonely words dangling on a separate line:
Penetration   significantly   3cu. In

?

This vague pronoun reference "it" alludes to *damage
to the left wing,* which caused the destruction of the
Columbia. The slide weakens important material with
ambiguous language (sentence fragments, passive voice,
multiple meanings of "significant"). The 3 reports
were created by engineers for high-level NASA officials
who were deciding whether the threat of wing damage
required further investigation before the Columbia
attempted to return. Satisfied that the reports indicated
that the Columbia was not in danger, the officials made
no further attempts to assess the threat. The slides were
part of an oral presentation, later circulated as e-mail
attachments.

In this slide the same unit of measure for volume
(cubic inches) is shown a different way every time
        3cu. In   1920cu in   3 cu in
rather than in clear and tidy exponential form **1920 in^3**.
Perhaps the available font cannot show exponents.
Shakiness in conventions for units of measurement should
provoke concern.* Slides with hierarchical bullet-outlines
do not handle statistical data and scientific notation
gracefully. If PowerPoint is a corporate-mandated format
for all engineering reports, then some competent scientific
typography (rather than the PP market-pitch style) is
essential. In this slide, the typography is so choppy and
clunky that it impedes understanding.

In the reports, *every single text-slide* uses bullet-outlines with 4 to 6 levels of hierarchy. Then another multi-level list, another bureaucracy of bullets, *starts afresh* for a new slide. How is it that each elaborate architecture of thought always fits *exactly* on one slide? The rigid slide-by-slide hierarchies, indifferent to content, slice and dice the evidence into arbitrary compartments, producing an anti-narrative with choppy continuity. Medieval in its preoccupation with hierarchical distinctions, the PowerPoint format signals every bullet's status in 4 or 5 different simultaneous ways: by the order in sequence, extent of indent, size of bullet, style of bullet, and size of type associated with various bullets. This is certainly a lot of format for a simple engineering problem.

This approach also makes a common error in design: information architectures mimic the hierarchical structure of the bureaucracy producing those architectures. Indeed, the report of the Columbia Accident Investigation Board suggests that the distinctive cognitive style of PowerPoint reinforced the hierarchical filtering and biases of the NASA bureaucracy during the crucial period when the Columbia was injured but still alive:

> The Mission Management Team Chair's position in the hierarchy governed what information she would or would not receive. Information was lost as it traveled up the hierarchy. A demoralized Debris Assessment Team did not include a slide about the need for better imagery in their presentation to the Mission Evaluation Room. Their presentation included the Crater analysis, which they reported as incomplete and uncertain. However, the Mission Evaluation Room manager perceived the Boeing analysis as rigorous and quantitative. The choice of headings, arrangement of information, and size of bullets on the key chart served to highlight what management already believed. The uncertainties and assumptions that signaled danger dropped out of the information chain when the Mission Evaluation Room manager condensed the Debris Assessment Team's formal presentation to an informal verbal brief at the Mission Management Team meeting.[5]

[5] Columbia Accident Investigation Board, *Report*, volume 1 (August 2003), p. 201.

At the same time, lower-level NASA engineers were writing about the possible danger to the Columbia in several hundred e-mails (with the Boeing reports in PP format sometimes attached). The text of 90% of these e-mails simply used paragraphs and sentences; 10% used bullet lists with 2 or 3 levels. That is, the engineers were able to reason about the issues without employing the multi-level hierarchical outlines of the original PP pitches.

Do complicated topics require ever more layered bullet structures? Scientists and engineers—and everyone else for that matter—have communicated about complex matters for centuries without hierarchical bullet outlines. Richard Feynman wrote about much of basic physics—mechanics, optics, thermodynamics, quantum behavior—in a 600-page book with *only 2 levels*: chapters and headings within chapters. ⟶

Below, page layout in Richard P. Feynman, Robert B. Leighton, and Matthew Sands, *The Feynman Lectures on Physics* (1963), chapter 38, page 5.

Richard Feynman had also experienced the bullet-outline format style of NASA in his service on the commission that investigated the first shuttle accident, the Challenger in 1986. Feynman wrote:

> Then we learned about "bullets"—little black circles in front of phrases that were supposed to summarize things. There was one after another of these little goddamn bullets in our briefing books and on slides.[6]

For some scientists and engineers, Feynman might serve as the decisive authority on this matter. Indeed, for those who have read Feynman's books, a good way to try to think clearly about evidence and explanation is to ask "What would Feynman do?"

The analysis of the key Columbia slide (shown here on pages 8-9) was posted at my website in March 2003.[7] Nearly all this material was then included by the Columbia Accident Investigation Board in their final report published in August 2003. In a section called "Engineering by Viewgraphs," the Board went quite beyond my case study of the key PP slide with these extraordinary remarks:

> As information gets passed up an organization hierarchy, from people who do analysis to mid-level managers to high-level leadership, key explanations and supporting information is filtered out. In this context, it is easy to understand how a senior manager might read this PowerPoint slide and not realize that it addresses a life-threatening situation.
>
> At many points during its investigation, the Board was surprised to receive similar presentation slides from NASA officials in place of technical reports. The Board views the endemic use of PowerPoint briefing slides instead of technical papers as an illustration of the problematic methods of technical communication at NASA.[8]

Clearly the Board had their fill of lightweight PP presentations!

For the Boeing PowerPoint reports and for the many PP presentations by NASA to the Board, the hierarchical bullet-outline failed to bring clarity, focus, or credibility to the presentations. On the contrary, the argument and evidence appeared broken up into small, arbitrary and misleading fragments.

And the *Harvard Business Review* study of corporate planning found that the widely used bullet outlines did not bring intellectual discipline to planning—instead the bullets accommodated the generic, superficial, and simplistic.

PowerPoint will not do for serious presentations. Serious problems require serious tools. Indeed, presenters may instantly damage their credibility by using PP for serious problems—as was the case for the NASA officials with their PP pitches and PP decks so naively presented to the very serious Columbia Accident Investigation Board.

[6] Richard P. Feynman, *"What Do You Care What Other People Think?"* (New York, 1988), pp. 126-127.

[7] "Columbia Evidence—Analysis of Key Slide," March 18, 2003, Ask E.T. Forum, www.edwardtufte.com

[8] Columbia Accident Investigation Board, *Report*, volume 1 (August 2003), p. 191.

High-Resolution Visual Channels Are Compromised by PowerPoint

A talk, which proceeds at a pace of 100 to 160 spoken words per minute, is not an especially high resolution method of data transmission. Rates of transmitting *visual* evidence can be far higher. The artist Ad Reinhardt said, "As for a picture, if it isn't worth a thousand words, the hell with it." People can quickly look over tables with hundreds of numbers in, say, financial or sports pages in newspapers. People read 300 to 1,000 printed words a minute, and find their way around a printed map or a 35mm slide displaying 5 to 40 MB in the visual field. Often the visual channel is an intensely high-resolution channel.

Yet, in a strange reversal, nearly all PowerPoint slides that accompany talks have much *lower* rates of information transmission than the talk itself. Too often the images are content-free clip art, the statistical graphics don't show data, and the text is grossly impoverished. As shown in this table, *the PowerPoint slide typically shows 40 words, which is about 8 seconds-worth of silent reading material.* The slides in PP textbooks are particularly disturbing: in 28 textbooks, which should use only first-rate examples, the median number of words per slide is 15, worthy of billboards, about 3 or 4 seconds of silent reading material.

This poverty of content has several sources. First, *the PP design style,* which typically uses only about 30% to 40% of the space available on a slide to show unique content, with all remaining space devoted to Phluff, bullets, frames, and branding. Second, the *slide projection of text,* which requires very large type so the audience can read the words. Third, *presenters who don't have all that much to say* (for example, among the 2,140 slides reported in our table, the really lightweight slides are found in the presentations made by educational administrators).

A vicious circle results. Thin content leads to boring presentations. To make them unboring, PP Phluff is added, damaging the content, making the presentation even more boring, requiring more Phluff . . . .

What to do? For serious presentations, it will be useful to replace PowerPoint slides with paper handouts showing words, numbers, data graphics, images together. High-resolution handouts allow viewers to contextualize, compare, narrate, and recast evidence. In contrast, data-thin, forgetful displays tend to make audiences ignorant and passive, and also to diminish the credibility of the presenter. Thin visual content prompts suspicions: "What are they leaving out? Is that all they know? Does the speaker think we're stupid?" "What are they hiding?" Sometimes PowerPoint's low resolution is said to promote a clarity of reading and thinking. Yet in visual reasoning, art, typography, cartography, even sculpture, *the quantity of detail is an issue completely separate from the difficulty of reading.*[9] Indeed, at times, the more intense the detail, the *greater* the clarity and understanding—because meaning and reasoning are *contextual.* Less is a bore.

WORDS ON TEXT-ONLY POWERPOINT SLIDES

26 slides in the 3 Columbia reports by Boeing, median number of words per slide	97
1,460 text-only slides in 189 PP reports posted on the internet and top-ranked by Google, March 2003, median number of words per slide	40
654 slides in 28 PowerPoint textbooks, published 1997–2003, median number of words per slide	15

[9] Edward R. Tufte, *Envisioning Information* (1990), pp. 36–51.

Metaphors for Presentations

Years before today's slideware, presentations at companies such as IBM and in the military used bullet lists shown by overhead projectors. Then, in 1984, a software house developed a presentation package, "Presenter," which was eventually acquired by Microsoft and turned into PowerPoint.

This history is revealing, for the metaphor behind the PP cognitive style is *the software corporation itself.* That is, a big bureaucracy engaged in *computer programming* (deeply hierarchical, nested, highly structured, relentlessly sequential, one-short-line-at-a-time) and in *marketing* (fast pace, misdirection, advocacy not analysis, slogan thinking, branding, exaggerated claims, marketplace ethics). *To describe a software house is to describe the PowerPoint cognitive style.* Why should the structure, activities, and values of a large commercial bureaucracy be a useful metaphor for our presentations? Could any metaphor be worse? Voice-mail menu systems? Billboards? Television? Stalin?

The pushy PP style imposes itself on the audience and, at times, seeks to set up a dominance relationship between speaker and audience. The speaker, after all, is making *power points with bullets to followers.* Such aggressive, stereotyped, over-managed presentations—the Great Leader up on the pedestal—are characteristic of hegemonic systems:

> The Roman state bolstered its authority and legitimacy with the trappings of ceremony. . . . Power is a far more complex and mysterious quality than any apparently simple manifestation of it would appear. It is as much a matter of impression, of theatre, of persuading those over whom authority is wielded to collude in their subjugation. Insofar as power is a matter of presentation, its cultural currency in antiquity (and still today) was the creation, manipulation, and display of images. In the propagation of the imperial office, at any rate, art was power.[10]

A better metaphor for presentations is *good teaching.*[11] Teachers seek to explain something with credibility, which is what many presentations are trying to do. The core ideas of teaching—*explanation, reasoning, finding things out, questioning, content, evidence, credible authority not patronizing authoritarianism*—are contrary to the hierarchical market-pitch approach.

Especially disturbing is the introduction of the PowerPoint cognitive style into schools. Instead of writing a report using sentences, children learn how to make client pitches and info-mercials, which is better than encouraging children to smoke. Elementary school PP exercises (as seen in teacher's guides, and in student work posted on the internet) typically show 10 to 20 words and a piece of clip art on each slide in a presentation consisting of 3 to 6 slides—a total of perhaps 80 words (15 seconds of silent reading) for a week of work. Rather than being trained as mini-bureaucrats in PPPhluff and foreshortening of thought, students would be better off if the schools simply closed down on those days and everyone went to The Exploratorium. Or wrote an illustrated essay explaining something.

[10] Jás Elsner, *Imperial Rome and Christian Triumph: The Art of the Roman Empire AD 100-450* (1998), p. 53.

[11] For various and sometimes divergent ideas about teaching and presentations, see Joseph Lowman, *Mastering the Techniques of Teaching* (1995); Wilbert J. McKeachie and Barbara K. Hofer, *McKeachie's Teaching Tips* (2001); Frederick Mosteller, "Classroom and Platform Performance," *The American Statistician,* 34 (February 1980), 11-17 (posted at www.edwardtufte.com); and Edward R. Tufte, *Visual Explanations* (1997), pp. 68-71.

The Gettysburg PowerPoint Presentation

The PP cognitive style is so distinctive and peculiar that presentations relying on standard ready-made templates sometimes appear as over-the-top parodies instead of the sad realities they are. Here is an intentional and ferocious parody: imagine Abraham Lincoln had used PowerPoint at Gettysburg. . . .

Um, my name is Abraham Lincoln and, um, I have to reboot . . . .

As we see in the Organizational Overview slide, four score and seven years ago our fathers brought forth on this continent a new nation, conceived in liberty and dedicated to the proposition that all men are created equal. Now we are engaged in a great civil war, testing whether that nation or any nation so conceived and so dedicated can long endure. Next slide please. We are met on a great battlefield of that war. We have come to dedicate a portion of that field as a final resting place for those who here gave their lives that that nation might live. It is altogether fitting and proper that we should do this. But in a larger sense, we cannot dedicate, we cannot consecrate, we cannot hallow this ground. The brave men, living and dead who struggled here have consecrated it far above our poor power to add or detract. Next slide please. The world will little note nor long remember what we say here, but it can never forget what they did here. It is for us the living rather to be dedicated here to the unfinished work which they who fought here have thus far so

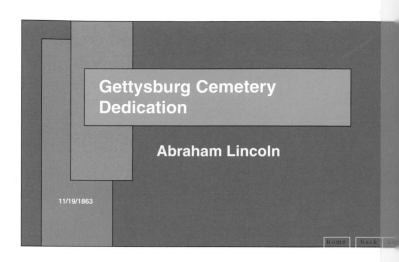

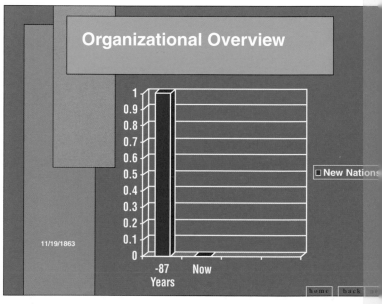

nobly advanced. It is rather for us to be here dedicated to the great task remaining before us— that from these honored dead we take increased devotion to that cause for which they gave the last full measure of devotion, that we here highly resolve that these dead shall not have died in vain, that this nation under God shall have a new birth of freedom, and that government of the people, by the people, for the people, next slide please, shall not perish from the earth.

This PowerPoint presentation was created by Peter Norvig; see www.norvig.com. Norvig notes that these slides were quickly constructed by means of the PP "AutoContent Wizard."

Just fancy that, "AutoContent." In an essay in *The New Yorker* (May 28, 2001), Ian Parker describes the AutoContent Wizard as "a rare example of a product named in outright mockery of its target customers" (p. 76).

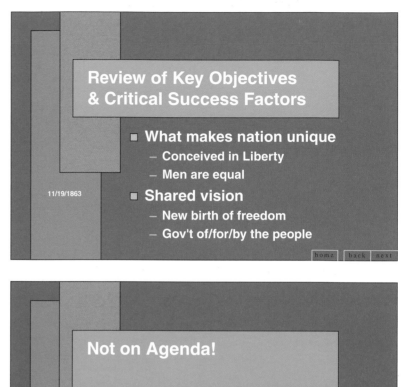

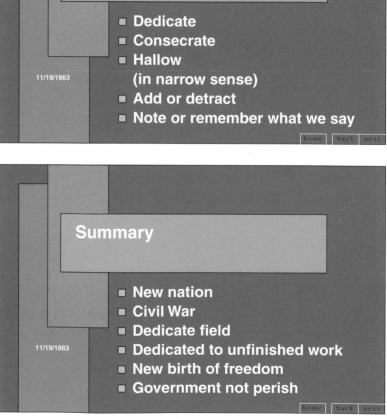

PowerPoint and Statistical Evidence

To investigate the performance of PP for statistical data, let us consider an important and intriguing table of cancer survival rates relative to those without cancer for the same time period. Some 196 numbers and 57 words describe survival rates and their standard errors for 24 cancers:

Estimates of relative survival rates, by cancer site[12]

	% survival rates and their standard errors			
	5 year	10 year	15 year	20 year
Prostate	98.8 0.4	95.2 0.9	87.1 1.7	81.1 3.0
Thyroid	96.0 0.8	95.8 1.2	94.0 1.6	95.4 2.1
Testis	94.7 1.1	94.0 1.3	91.1 1.8	88.2 2.3
Melanomas	89.0 0.8	86.7 1.1	83.5 1.5	82.8 1.9
Breast	86.4 0.4	78.3 0.6	71.3 0.7	65.0 1.0
Hodgkin's disease	85.1 1.7	79.8 2.0	73.8 2.4	67.1 2.8
Corpus uteri, uterus	84.3 1.0	83.2 1.3	80.8 1.7	79.2 2.0
Urinary, bladder	82.1 1.0	76.2 1.4	70.3 1.9	67.9 2.4
Cervix, uteri	70.5 1.6	64.1 1.8	62.8 2.1	60.0 2.4
Larynx	68.8 2.1	56.7 2.5	45.8 2.8	37.8 3.1
Rectum	62.6 1.2	55.2 1.4	51.8 1.8	49.2 2.3
Kidney, renal pelvis	61.8 1.3	54.4 1.6	49.8 2.0	47.3 2.6
Colon	61.7 0.8	55.4 1.0	53.9 1.2	52.3 1.6
Non-Hodgkin's	57.8 1.0	46.3 1.2	38.3 1.4	34.3 1.7
Oral cavity, pharynx	56.7 1.3	44.2 1.4	37.5 1.6	33.0 1.8
Ovary	55.0 1.3	49.3 1.6	49.9 1.9	49.6 2.4
Leukemia	42.5 1.2	32.4 1.3	29.7 1.5	26.2 1.7
Brain, nervous system	32.0 1.4	29.2 1.5	27.6 1.6	26.1 1.9
Multiple myeloma	29.5 1.6	12.7 1.5	7.0 1.3	4.8 1.5
Stomach	23.8 1.3	19.4 1.4	19.0 1.7	14.9 1.9
Lung and bronchus	15.0 0.4	10.6 0.4	8.1 0.4	6.5 0.4
Esophagus	14.2 1.4	7.9 1.3	7.7 1.6	5.4 2.0
Liver, bile duct	7.5 1.1	5.8 1.2	6.3 1.5	7.6 2.0
Pancreas	4.0 0.5	3.0 1.5	2.7 0.6	2.7 0.8

Applying the PowerPoint templates for statistical graphics to this nice straightforward table yields the analytical disasters on the facing page. "Sweet songs never last too long on broken radios," wrote John Prine. These PP default-designs cause the data to explode into 6 separate chaotic slides, consuming 2.9 times the area of the table. *Everything* is wrong with these smarmy, incoherent graphs: uncomparative, thin data-density, chartjunk, encoded legends, meaningless color, logotype branding, indifferent to content and evidence. Chartjunk is a clear sign of statistical stupidity; use these designs in your presentation, and your audience will quickly and correctly conclude that you don't know much about data and evidence.[13] Poking a finger into the eye of thought, these data graphics would turn into a nasty travesty if used for

[12] Redesigned table based on Hermann Brenner, "Long-term survival rates of cancer patients achieved by the end of the 20th century: a period analysis," *The Lancet,* 360 (October 12, 2002), 1131–1135. Brenner recalculates survival rates from data collected by the U.S. National Cancer Institute, 1973–1998, from the Surveillance, Epidemiology, and End Results Program.

[13] PP-style chartjunk occasionally shows up in graphics of evidence in scientific journals. Below, the clutter half-conceals thin data with some vibrating pyramids framed by an unintentional Necker illusion, as the 2 back planes optically flip to the front:

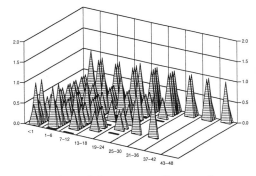

For such small data sets, usually a simple table will show the data more effectively than a graph, let alone a chartjunk graph. Source of graph: N. T. Kouchoukos, *et al.,* "Replacement of the Aortic Root with a Pulmonary Autograft in Children and Young Adults with Aortic-Valve Disease," *New England Journal of Medicine,* 330 (January 6, 1994), p. 4. On chartjunk, see Edward R. Tufte, *The Visual Display of Quantitative Information* (1983, 2001), chapter 5.

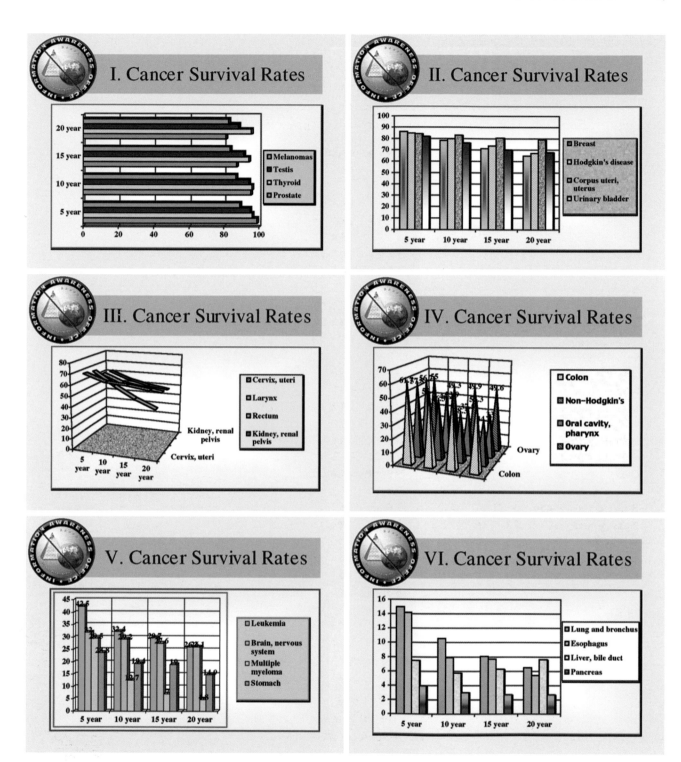

a serious purpose, such as cancer patients seeking to assess their survival chances. To deal with a product that messes up data with such systematic intensity must require an enormous insulation from statistical integrity and statistical reasoning by Microsoft PP executives and programmers, PP textbook writers, and presenters of such chartjunk.

The best way to show the cancer data is the original table with its good comparative structure and reporting of standard errors. And PP default graphics are not the way to see the data. Our table-graphic, however, does give something of a *visual idea* of time-gradients for survival for each cancer. Like the original table, every visual element in the graphic shows data. Slideware displays, in contrast, usually devote a majority of their space to things other than data.

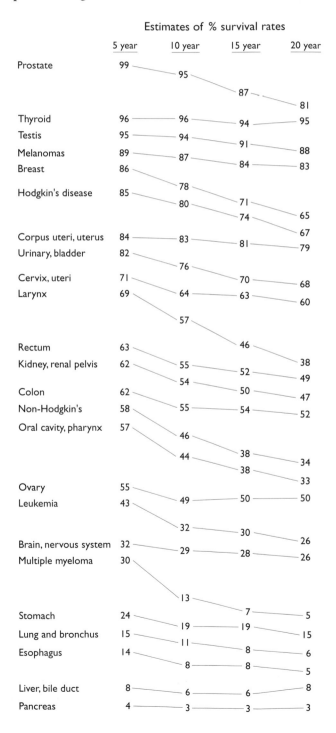

Estimates of % survival rates

	5 year	10 year	15 year	20 year
Prostate	99	95	87	81
Thyroid	96	96	94	95
Testis	95	94	91	88
Melanomas	89	87	84	83
Breast	86	78	71	65
Hodgkin's disease	85	80	74	67
Corpus uteri, uterus	84	83	81	79
Urinary, bladder	82	76	70	68
Cervix, uteri	71	64	63	60
Larynx	69	57	46	38
Rectum	63	55	52	49
Kidney, renal pelvis	62	54	50	47
Colon	62	55	54	52
Non-Hodgkin's	58	46	38	34
Oral cavity, pharynx	57	44	38	33
Ovary	55	49	50	50
Leukemia	43	32	30	26
Brain, nervous system	32	29	28	26
Multiple myeloma	30	13	7	5
Stomach	24	19	19	15
Lung and bronchus	15	11	8	6
Esophagus	14	8	8	5
Liver, bile duct	8	6	6	8
Pancreas	4	3	3	3

PowerPoint Stylesheets

The PP cognitive style is propagated by the templates, textbooks, stylesheets, and complete pitches available for purchase. Some corporations and government agencies *require* employees to use designated PPPhluff and presentation logo-wear. With their strict generic formats, these designer stylesheets serve only to enforce the limitations of PowerPoint, compromising the presenter, the content, and, ultimately, the audience.

Here we see a witless PP pitch on how to make a witless PP pitch. Prepared at the Harvard School of Public Health by the "Instructional Computing Facility," these templates are uninformed by the practices of scientific publication and the rich intellectual history of evidence and analysis in public health. The templates do, however, emulate the format of reading primers for 6 year-olds.

Jane said, "Here is a ball.
See this blue ball, Sally.
Do you want this ball?"

Sally said, "I want my ball.
My ball is yellow.
It is a big, pretty ball."

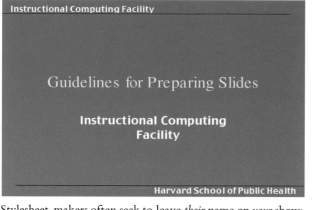

Stylesheet-makers often seek to leave *their* name on *your* show; "branding," as they say in the Marketing Department. In case you didn't notice, this presentation is from the "Instructional Computing Facility." But where are the names of the people responsible for this? No names appear on any of the 21 slides.

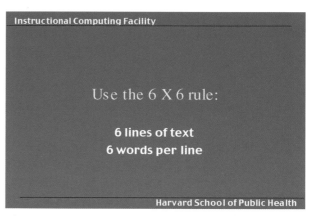

This must be the Haiku Rule for formatting scientific lectures. At least we're not limited to 17 syllables per slide. Above this slide, the rule can be seen in action—in a first-grade reading primer. The stylesheet typography, distinctly unscientific, uses a capital X instead of a multiplication sign.

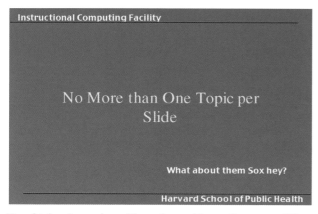

But this breaks up the evidence into arbitrary fragments. Why aren't we seeing examples from actual scientific reports? What are the Sox (a rather parochial reference) doing here? The inept PP typography persists: strange over-active indents, oddly chosen initial caps, typographic orphans on 3 of 4 slides.

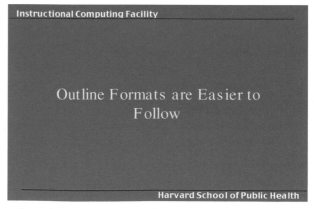

Why is this relevant to scientific presentations? Are there other principles than ease of following? Didn't the *Harvard Business Review* article indicate that bullet outlines corrupted thought? Text, imaging, and data for scientific presentations should be at the level of scientific journals, much *higher* resolution than speech.

20

Instructional Computing Facility

Use Simple Tables to Present Numbers

	Use Tables	For Your Numbers	But Not too Many
This row	10	90	100
This row	0.6	0.4	1
This row	1	2	3
That row	1	2	3

Try not to make footnotes too small

Harvard School of Public Health

The stylesheet goes on to victimize statistical data, the fundamental evidence of public health. The table shows 12 numbers which is lousy for science (or sports, or finance) but normal for PowerPoint.[14] Table design is a complex and intriguing matter in typographic work, but there is nothing thoughtful about the design here. The unsourced numbers are not properly aligned, the row and column labels are awful, the units of measurement not given. In this stylesheet, there lurks a casual, flippant, almost smirky attitude toward data. That attitude—*what counts are power and pitches, not truth and evidence*—also lurks within PowerPoint.

Consider now a real table. John Graunt's *Bills of Mortality* (1662) is the foundation work of public health, introducing scientific methods to medical and demographic data. Graunt calculated the first tables of life expectancy, compared different causes of death, and even discussed defects in the evidence. His renowned "Table of Casualties" (at right) shows 1,855 different counts of death from 1629 to 1659. How fortunate that Graunt did not have PowerPoint and the assistance of the Harvard School of Public Health Instructional Computing Facility. Their guidelines (above) imply the construction of 155 separate PowerPoint slides to show the data in Graunt's original table!

For tables, the analytical idea is to make comparisons. The number of possible pairwise comparisons in a table increases as the square of the number of cells.[15] In Graunt's table, 1,719,585 pairwise comparisons, of varying relevance to be sure, are within the eyespan of the inquiring mind. In contrast, the 155 tiny tables on 155 PP slides would offer only 10,230 pairwise comparisons, about 6 in 1,000 of those available in Graunt's original table. These PP tables would also block all sorts of interesting comparisons, such as time patterns over many years. What Graunt needs to do for his presentation at Harvard is simply to provide printed copies of his original table to everyone in the audience.

[14] Some 39 tables appear in our collection of 28 PP textbooks. These tables show an average (median) of 12 numbers each, which approaches the *Pravda* level. In contrast, sports and financial pages in newspapers routinely present tables with hundreds, even thousands of numbers. Below, we see a simple weather table from a newspaper. The Harvard School of Public Health claims that to show this information would require 31 separate PowerPoint slides!

Africa	Yesterday	Today	Tomorrow
Algiers	82/ 66 0.55	85/ 60 S	85/ 61 S
Cairo	99/ 70 0	101/ 76 S	96/ 76 S
Cape Town	64/ 54 0.16	63/ 49 PC	60/ 50 Sh
Dakar	87/ 77 0.75	86/ 81 PC	85/ 81 PC
Johannesburg	69/ 42 0	73/ 42 S	71/ 47 S
Nairobi	75/ 55 0	78/ 56 PC	78/ 56 PC
Tunis	80/ 69 –	87/ 73 PC	85/ 71 PC
Asia/Pacific	Yesterday	Today	Tomorrow
Auckland	59/ 45 0.12	58/ 44 Sh	58/ 44 Sh
Bangkok	91/ 82 0	91/ 79 Sh	91/ 77 Sh
Beijing	85/ 57 0	84/ 60 S	78/ 65 PC
Bombay	88/ 75 0.28	87/ 77 T	88/ 78 T
Damascus	96/ 55 0	98/ 59 S	96/ 62 S
Hong Kong	91/ 77 0	88/ 81 PC	92/ 78 PC
Jakarta	89/ 77 0	90/ 77 PC	89/ 77 PC
Jerusalem	87/ 64 0	88/ 66 S	88/ 69 S
Karachi	86/ 80 0	92/ 78 PC	92/ 79 S
Manila	86/ 75 –	84/ 75 R	87/ 78 R
New Delhi	89/ 80 Tr	88/ 76 Sh	92/ 76 Sh
Riyadh	98/ 69 0	102/ 74 S	101/ 75 S
Seoul	78/ 64 2.09	83/ 65 PC	77/ 66 R
Shanghai	75/ 69 0.06	86/ 76 Sh	86/ 73 PC
Singapore	87/ 78 Tr	89/ 76 R	89/ 78 Sh
Sydney	68/ 53 0	71/ 51 PC	71/ 48 PC
Taipei	84/ 77 2.28	87/ 73 PC	88/ 72 PC
Tehran	93/ 73 0	87/ 73 S	87/ 73 S
Tokyo	89/ 77 0	91/ 79 Sh	83/ 80 Sh
Europe	Yesterday	Today	Tomorrow
Amsterdam	56/ 50 0.39	66/ 51 PC	64/ 52 Sh
Athens	87/ 75 0	90/ 75 S	88/ 71 S
Berlin	64/ 55 0.31	61/ 49 R	68/ 52 PC
Brussels	62/ 54 Tr	66/ 53 PC	65/ 52 Sh
Budapest	72/ 59 0	75/ 55 S	67/ 53 Sh
Copenhagen	59/ 51 0.08	63/ 51 Sh	63/ 52 PC
Dublin	66/ 54 0.12	66/ 55 Sh	63/ 47 PC
Edinburgh	63/ 46 0.02	63/ 46 R	64/ 48 PC
Frankfurt	65/ 54 0.01	65/ 54 Sh	66/ 50 PC
Geneva	69/ 57 0.04	64/ 56 Sh	65/ 50 PC
Helsinki	63/ 45 0	62/ 46 PC	63/ 45 PC
Istanbul	84/ 60 0.01	79/ 69 Sh	78/ 67 S
Kiev	66/ 46 0	64/ 47 S	64/ 46 S
Lisbon	84/ 62 0	91/ 65 S	90/ 67 S
London	71/ 53 0.08	66/ 53 Sh	69/ 55 PC
Madrid	86/ 46 0	87/ 55 S	87/ 57 S
Moscow	55/ 41 0	64/ 40 S	62/ 44 S
Nice	78/ 62 0.01	78/ 65 S	78/ 63 S
Oslo	62/ 48 0	57/ 47 PC	59/ 45 PC
Paris	68/ 57 0	69/ 56 PC	68/ 57 PC
Prague	64/ 55 0.04	56/ 49 T	63/ 49 Sh
Rome	75/ 62 –	79/ 61 S	76/ 60 Sh
St. Petersburg	59/ 39 0	66/ 46 S	65/ 47 PC
Stockholm	64/ 46 0	61/ 49 PC	63/ 45 PC
Vienna	64/ 59 0.16	65/ 53 PC	66/ 52 PC
Warsaw	69/ 46 0	62/ 51 Sh	65/ 49 PC

[15] A table with n cells yields $n(n-1)/2$ pairwise comparisons of cell entries.

John Graunt, *National and Political Observations mentioned in a following index, and made upon the Bills of Mortality. With reference to the Government, Religion, Trade, Growth, Ayre, Diseases, and the several Changes of the said City* (London, 1662). "The Table of Casualties" follows folio 74.

THE TABLE OF CASUALTIES.

The Years of our Lord	1647	1648	1649	1650	1651	1652	1653	1654	1655	1656	1657	1658	1659	1660	1629	1630	1631	1632	1633	1634	1635	1636	1629 1630 1631 1632	1633 1634 1635 1636	1647 1648 1649 1650	1651 1652 1653 1654	1655 1656 1657 1658	1629 1649 1659	In 20 Years
rtive, and ftilborn	335	329	327	351	389	381	384	433	483	419	463	467	421	544	499	439	410	445	500	475	507	523	1793	2005	1342	1587	1832	1247	8559
d	916	835	889	696	780	834	864	974	743	892	869	1176	909	1095	579	712	661	671	704	623	794	714	2475	2814	3336	3452	3680	2377	15757
e, and Fever	1260	884	751	970	1038	1212	1282	1371	689	875	999	1800	2303	2148	956	1091	1115	1108	953	1279	1622	2360	4418	6235	3865	4903	4363	4010	23784
plex, and fodainly	68	74	64	74	106	111	118	86	92	102	113	138	91	67	22	36			17	24	35	26	75	85	280	421	445	177	1306
ch			1		3	7	2			1															4	9	1	1	15
ted	4	1			6	6		4		5	5	3	8	13	8	10	13	6	4		4		54	14	5	12	14	16	99
ding	3	2	5	1	3	4	3	2	7	3	5	4	7	2	5	2	5	4	4	3			16	7	11	12	19	17	65
dy Flux, Scouring, and Flux	155	176	802	289	833	762	200	386	168	368	362	233	346	251	449	438	352	348	278	512	346	330	1587	1466	1422	2181	1161	1597	7818
nt, and Scalded	3	6	10	5	11	8	5	7	10	5	7	4	6	4	6	3	10	7	5	1	3		25	19	24	31	26	19	125
enture	1			1		2	1	1				3							1	3					4	2	4	3	13
cer, Gangrene, and Fiftula	26	29	31	19	31	53	36	37	73	31	24	35	63	52	20	14	23	28	27	30	24	30	85	112	105	157	150	114	609
f																						8							8
ker, Sore-mouth, and Thrufh	66	28	54	42	68	51	53	72	44	81	19	27	73	68	6	4	4	1			5	74	15	79	190	244	161	133	689
dbed	161	106	114	117	206	213	158	192	177	201	236	225	226	194	150	157	112	171	132	143	163	230	590	668	498	769	839	490	3364
ifomes, and Infants	1369	1254	1065	990	1237	1280	1050	1343	1089	1393	1162	1144	858	1123	2596	2378	2035	2268	2130	2315	2113	1895	9277	8453	4678	4910	4788	4519	32106
ck, and Wind	103	71	85	82	76	102		80	101	85	120	113	179	116	167	48	57			37	50	105	87	341	359	497	247		1389
d, and Cough							41	36	21	58	30	31	33	24	10	58	51	55	45	54	50	57	174	207	00	77	140	43	598
nfumption, and Cough	2423	2200	2388	1988	2350	2410	2286	2868	2606	3184	2757	3610	2982	3414	1827	1910	1713	1797	1754	1955	2080	2477	5157	8266	8999	9914	12157	7197	44487
vulsion	684	491	530	493	569	653	606	828	702	1027	807	841	742	1031	52	87	18	241	221	386	418	709	498	1734	2198	2656	3377	1324	9073
mp			1																	5	1	5	2	5	10	6	4	13	47
of the Stone			2	1	3		1		2	4	1	3			1	0	0	0	0	0					6	4	13	47	2
pfy, and Tympany	185	434	421	508	444	556	617	704	660	706	631	931	646	872	235	252	279	280	266	250	329	389	048	1734	1538	2321	2982	1302	9623
wned	47	40	30	27	49	50	53	30	43	45	63	60	57	48	43	33	29	34	37	32	32	45	139	147	144	182	215	130	827
effive drinking			2																						2				2
cuted	8	17	29	43	24	12	19	21	19	22	20	18	7	18	19	13	12	18	13	13	13		62	52	97	76	79	55	384
ted in a Bath					1																				1				1
ng-Sicknefs	3	2	2	3	1	3	4	1	4	3	5	4	3	10	7	7	2	6	8	27	10	8	8	9					74
x, and fmall pox	139	400	1190	184	525	1279	139	812	1294	823	835	409	1523	354	72	40	58	531	72	1354	293	127	701	1846	1913	2755	3361	2785	10576
nd dead in the Streets	6	6	9	8	7	9	14	4	3	4	9	11	2	6	18	33	26	6	13	8	24	83	69	29	34	27	29		243
nch-Pox	18	29	15	18	21	20	20	20	29	23	25	53	51	31	17	12	12	12	7	17	12	22	53	48	80	81	130	83	392
hted	4	4	1		3		2		1	1			9		1			1					3	2	3	9	5	2	21
ut	9	5	12	9	7	7	5	6	8	7	8	13	14		2	5	3	4	4	5	7	8	14	24	35	25	36	28	134
ef	12	13	16	7	17	14	11	17	10	13	10	12	13	4	18	20	22	11	14	17	5	20	71	56	48	59	45	47	279
ged, and made-away themfelves	11	10	13	14	9	14	15	9	14	16	24	18	11	36	8	6	15				3	8	7	37	48	47	72	32	222
d-Ach		1	11	2		2	6	5		3	4	5	35	26								4	2	0	6	14	14	17 46	051
ndice	57	35	39	49	41	43	57	71	61	41	46	77	102	76	47	59	35	43	35	45	54	63	184	197	180	212	225	188	998
-faln	1	1			3				2	2		3	1		10	16	13	8	10	10	4	11	47	35	00	5	6	10	95
oftume	75	61	65	59	80	105	79	90	92	122	80	134	105	96	58	76	73	74	50	62	73	130	282	315	260	354	428	228	1639
ed by feveral Accidents	27	57	39	94	47	45	57	58	52	43	52	47	55	47	54	55	47	46	49	41	51	60	202	201	217	207	194	148	1021
s Evil	27	26	22	19	22	20	26	26	27	24	23	28	28	54	16	25	18	38	35	20	26	69	97	150	94	94	102	66	537
hargy	3	4	2	4	4	4	3	10	9	4	6	2	6	4	1		2	2	3		2	2	5	7	13	21	21	9	67
rofy			1							1			1	2						2		2	2	1	1	1	3		06
ergrown, Spleen, and Rickets	53	46	56	59	65	72	67	65	52	50	38	51	8	15	94	112	99	87	82	77	98	99	392	356	213	269	191	158	1421
atique	12	18	6	11	7	11	9	12	6	7	13	5	14	14	6	11	6	5	4	2	5	28	13	47	39	31	26		158
agrom	12	13		5	8	6	6	14	3	6	7	6	5	4				24				22	24	22	30	34	22	05	132
afles	5	92	4	33	33	62	8	52	11	153	15	80	6	74	42	3	80	21	33		12	127	83	133	155	259	51		757
ther	2						1	1	2	1	2	3	3	1	1							01	1	4	2	8	02		18
rdered	3	2	7	5	4	3	3	3	9	6	5	7	70	20		3	7			6	5	8	10	19	17	13	27	77	86
erlayd, and ftarved at Nurfe	25	22	36	28	28	29	30	36	58	53	44	50	46	43	4	10	13	7	8	10	14	34	46	111	123	215	86		529
y	27	21	19	20	23	20	29	18	22	23	20	22	17	21	17	23	17	25	14	21	25	17	82	77	87	90	87	53	423
gue	3597	611	67	15	23	16	6	16	9	6	4	14	36	14	1317	274	8		1			10400	1599	10401	4290	61	33	103	16384
gue in the Guts				1		110	32			37	315	446		253	402								00	00	61	142	844	253	991
rify	30	26	13	20	23	19	17	23	10	9	17	16	12	10	26	24	26	36	21		45	24	112	90	89	72	52	51	415
foned		3		7														2			2	00	4	10	00	00			14
ples, and fpotted Fever	145	47	43	65	54	60	75	89	56	52	56	126	368	146	32	58	58	38	24	125	245	397	186	791	300	278	290	243	1845
nfy, and Sore-throat	14	11	12	17	24	20	18	9	15	13	7	10	21	14	01	8	6	7	24	04	5	22	22	55	54	71	45	34	247
kets	150	224	216	190	260	329	229	372	347	458	317	476	441	521							14	49	50	00	113	780	1190	1598 657	3681
ther, rifing of the Lights	150	92	115	120	134	138	135	178	166	212	203	228	210	249	44	72	99	98	60	84	72	104	309	220	777	585	809	369	2700
oture	16	7	7	6	7	16	7	15	11	20	19	18	12	28	2	6	4	9	4	3	10	13	21	30	36	45	68	2	201
'd-head	2				1				2														2	1	2				05
rvy	32	20	21	21	29	43	41	44	103	71	82	82	95	12	5	7			9			00	25	33	34	94	132	300 115	593
othered, and ftifled			2														24					24			2				26
es, Ulcers, broken and bruifed (Limbs	15	17	17	16	26	32	25	32	23	34	40	47	61	48 7 20	23		20	48	19	19	22	29	91	89	65	115	144	141 07	504 27
een	12	17					13	13		6	2	5	7	7				1					29	26	13	07			68
ngles													1	1														1	2
ved			4	8	7	1	2	1		3	1	3	6	7	14					14			19	5	13	29			51
ch				1																					1				1
ne, and Strangury	45	42	29	28	50	41	44	38	49	57	72	69	22	30				58	56	58	49	33	45	114	185	144	173	247 51	863
atica														2					1	3		1	6	1					15
pping of the Stomach	29	29	30	33	55	67	66	107	94	145	129	277	186	214								6		6	121	295	247	216	669
fet	217	137	136	123	104	177	178	212	128	161	137	218	202	192	63	157	149	86	104	114	132	371	445	721	613	671	644	401	3094
ne-Pox	4	4	3				1	4	2	1	1	1			5	8	4	6	3		10		23	13	11	5	5	10	57
th, and Worms	767	597	540	598	709	905	691	1131	803	1198	878	1036	839	1008	440	506	335	470	432	454	539	1207	1751	2632	2502	3436	3915	1819	14236
ick	62	47							57	66					8	12	14	34	23	15	27		68	65	109			8	242
ufh															15	23	17	40	28	31	34		95	93			123	15	211
miting	1	6	3		7	4	6	3	14	1	27	16	19	8 10	4	1	1	1	2	5	6	3	7	16	17	27	69	12	136
rms	147	107	105	65	85	86	53				1		1		19	31	28	27	19	28	27		105	74	424	224	45	124	830
ainly															63	59	37	62	58	62	78	34	221	233				63	454

Creeping PowerPoint: PP Slide Formats for Paper Reports and Computer Screens

In addition to outlining and accompanying a talk, PP slides often serve other functions—printed out on paper to make a report, attached to e-mails, posted on the internet. The PP slide format now shows up on paper and computer screen. These slides, especially those following ready-made templates, replicate and intensify all the problems of the PP cognitive style onto paper and computer screen. *Again the short-run convenience for the presenter (and for PowerPoint) comes at an enormous cost to the content and the audience.*

As those who have flipped through pages and pages and pages of printed out PP slides already know, such reports are physically thick and intellectually thin. Their resolution is remarkably low. The table at right compiles data comparing the information densities of one image-equivalent for books (one page), for the internet (one screen), and for PP (one slide). In terms of character density, printed reports in PP format typically perform at 2% to 10% of the typographic richness of nonfiction bestsellers! Looking from the top lines down to the bottom lines of the table, we see that a single printed page in the *Physicians' Desk Reference* shows more than 50 PP slide-equivalents of information.

People see, read, and think all the time at intensities vastly greater than those presented in printed PP reports. Instead of showing a long sequence of tiny information-fragments on slides, and instead of dumping those slides onto paper, report writers should have the courtesy to write a real report (which might also be handed out at a meeting) and address their readers as serious people. PP templates are a lazy and ridiculous way to format printed reports.

PP slides also format material on the internet. Presenters post their slides; then readers, if any, march through one slide after another on the computer screen. And you thought PP talks were incoherent. Popular news sites on the internet show 10 to 15 times more information on a computer screen than a typical PP slide posted on a computer screen. The shuttle Columbia reports prepared by Boeing, when sent around by e-mail in PP format, were running at information densities of 20% of news sites on the internet (table above right).

The PP slide format has probably the worst signal/noise ratio of any known method of communication on paper or computer screen. Extending PowerPoint to embrace paper and internet screens pollutes those display methods.

CHARACTER COUNTS AND DENSITY PER PAGE-IMAGE

	CHARACTERS PER PAGE	DENSITY: CHARACTERS/IN
BEST SELLING BOOKS		
Physicians' Desk Reference	13,600	168
Your Income Tax	10,400	118
World Almanac	9,800	232
Joy of Cooking	5,700	108
Baby and Child Care	2,500	95
The Merck Manual	4,700	42
Guinness Book of World Records	4,600	162
Consumer Reports Buying Guide	3,900	112
How to Cook Everything	3,900	53
Elmore Leonard, *Maximum Bob*	3,100	115
Carl Hiassen, *Basket Case*	2,800	104
NEWS SITES ON THE INTERNET		
Google News	4,100	44
New York Times	4,100	43
Los Angeles Times	4,000	42
MSN Slate	3,300	36
CNN	3,300	35
Yahoo	3,200	34
USA Today	2,700	29
Time	2,700	28
ABC News	2,500	27
MSNBC	2,400	26
POWERPOINT SLIDE FORMAT ON PAPER OR COMPUTER SCREEN		
Columbia reports by Boeing	630	7
1,460 text slides in 189 PP reports	250	3
654 text slides in 28 PP textbooks	98	1
Content-free slides	0	0

Sequentiality of the Slide Format

With information quickly appearing and disappearing, the slide transition is an event that attracts attention to the presentation's compositional methods. The slide serves up a small chunk of promptly vanishing information in a restless one-way sequence. It is not a contemplative analytical method; it is like television, or a movie with frequent random jump cuts. Sometimes quick chunks of thin data may be useful (flash-card memorizing), other times not (comparisons, links, explanations). *But formats, sequencing, and cognitive approach should be decided by the character of the content and what is to be explained, not by the limitations of the presentation technology.* The talk that accompanies PP slides may overcome the noise and clutter that results from slideville's arbitrary partitioning of data, but why disrupt the signal in the first place? And why should we need to recover from a technology that is supposed to help our presentations?

Obnoxious transitions and partitions occur not only slide-by-slide but also line-by-line. We have seen the problems with the bullet list. Worse is the method of line-by-line slow reveal (at right). Beginning with a title slide, the presenter unveils and reads aloud the single line on the slide, then reveals the next line, reads that aloud, on and on, as stupefied audience members impatiently await the end of the talk.

It is helpful to provide audience members with at least one mode of information that allows *them* to control the order and pace of learning—unlike slides and unlike talk. Paper handouts for talks will help provide a permanent record for review—again unlike projected images and talk. Another way to break free of low-resolution temporal comparisons is to show multiple slides, several images at once within the common view. Spatial parallelism takes advantage of our notable capacity to reason about multiple images that appear simultaneously within our eyespan. We are able to select, sort, edit, reconnoiter, review—ways of seeing quickened and sharpened by direct spatial adjacency of evidence.

Now and then the narrow bandwidth and relentless sequencing of slides are said to be virtues, a claim justified by loose reference to George Miller's classic 1956 paper "The Magical Number Seven, Plus or Minus Two." That essay reviews psychological experiments that discovered people had a hard time remembering more than about 7 unrelated pieces of really dull data all at once. These studies on memorizing nonsense then led some interface designers to conclude that only 7 items belong on a list or a slide, a conclusion that can only be reached by not reading Miller's paper. In fact the paper neither states nor implies rules for the amount of information to be shown in a presentation (except possibly for slides consisting of nonsense syllables that the audience must memorize and repeat back to a psychologist). Indeed, the deep point of Miller's work is to suggest strategies, such as placing information within a context, that help extend the reach of memory beyond tiny clumps of data.[16]

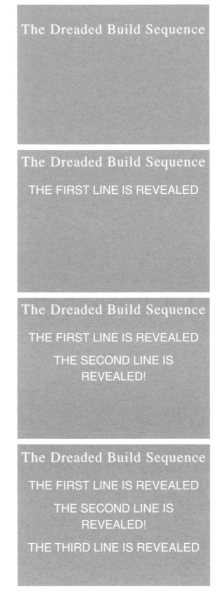

[THE AUDIENCE FLEES]

[16] George A. Miller, "The Magical Number Seven, Plus or Minus Two: Some Limits on Our Capacity for Processing Information," *Psychological Review,* 63 (1956), 81-97 (posted at www.well.com/user/smalin/miller.html). At Williams College in September 2000, I saw George Miller give a superb presentation that used the optimal number of bullet points on the optimal number of slides—zero in both cases. Just a nice straightforward talk with a long narrative structure.

What to do about PowerPoint

Imagine a widely used and expensive prescription drug that claimed to make us beautiful but didn't. Instead the drug had frequent, serious side effects: making us stupid, degrading the quality and credibility of our communication, turning us into bores, wasting our colleagues' time. These side effects, and the resulting unsatisfactory cost/benefit ratio, would rightly lead to a worldwide product recall.

Improving Our Presentations

Presentations largely stand or fall depending on the quality, relevance, and integrity of the content. The way to make big improvements in a presentation is to get better content.

Designer formats will not salvage weak content. If your numbers are boring, then you've got the wrong numbers. If your words or images are not on point, making them dance in color won't make them relevant. Audience boredom is usually a content failure, not a decoration failure.

At a minimum, a presentation format should *do no harm* to content. Yet again and again we have seen that the PP cognitive style routinely disrupts, dominates, and trivializes content. PP presentations too often resemble the school play: very loud, very slow, and very simple.

The practical conclusions are clear. PowerPoint is a competent slide manager and projector for low-resolution materials. And that's about it. PP has some occasionally useful low-end design tools and way too many Phluff tools. No matter how beautiful your PP ready-made template is, it would be better if there were less of it. Never use PP templates for arraying words or numbers. Avoid elaborate hierarchies of bullet lists. Never read aloud from slides. Never use PP templates to format paper reports or web screens. Use PP as a projector for showing low-resolution color images, graphics, and videos that cannot be reproduced as printed handouts at a presentation.

Paper handouts at a talk can effectively show text, numbers, data graphics, images. Printed materials, which should largely replace PP, bring information transfer rates in presentations up to that of everyday material in newspapers, magazines, books, and internet screens. A useful paper size for handouts at presentations is 11 by 17 inches (28 by 43 cm), folded in half to make 4 pages. This piece of paper can show images with a resolution of 1,200 dpi and up to 60,000 characters of words and numbers, the content-equivalent of 50 to 250 typical PP slides of text and data. Thoughtfully planned handouts at your talk tell the audience that you are serious and precise; that you seek to leave traces and have consequences. And that you respect your audience.

In day-to-day practice, PowerPoint templates may improve 10% or 20% of all presentations by organizing inept, extremely disorganized speakers, at a cost of detectable intellectual damage to 80%. For statistical data, the damage levels approach dementia. Since about 10^{10} to 10^{11} PP slides (many using the templates) are made each year, that is a lot of harm to communication with colleagues. Or at least a big waste of time.

The damage is mitigated since meetings relying on the PP cognitive style may not matter all that much. By playing around with Phluff rather than providing information, *PowerPoint allows speakers to pretend that they are giving a real talk, and audiences to pretend that they are listening.* This prankish conspiracy against substance and thought should always provoke the question, *Why are we having this meeting?*

As a consumer of presentations, you should not trust speakers who rely on the PP cognitive style. It is likely that these speakers are simply serving up PowerPointPhluff to mask their lousy content, just as this massive tendentious pedestal in Budapest once served up Stalin-cult propaganda to orderly followers feigning attention.

Military parade, Stalin Square, Budapest, April 4, 1956. Photograph by AP/Wide World Photos.

Postscript: Questions That Have Been Asked

The first printing of this essay, along with some brief excerpts in *Wired* magazine and at my website, provoked many comments and questions. Here are responses to the more important concerns.

The problem is with presenters who misuse PowerPoint. PowerPoint is just a tool; why blame the software for bad presentations? When a carpenter makes a crooked cut, do we blame the saw? Just because some people do silly things in PP doesn't mean that PP has a problem; people do silly things in written reports also.

This makes one good point: responsibility for poor presentations rests with the presenter. But it is more complicated than that. PP has a distinctive, definite, well-enforced, and widely-practiced cognitive style that is contrary to serious thinking. PP actively facilitates the making of lightweight presentations.

This essay reports evidence based on several thousand slides, 5 case studies, and extensive quantitative comparisons between PowerPoint and other methods of communicating information. The results are clear: *some methods of presentation are better than others. And PowerPoint is rarely a good method*. The Columbia Accident Investigation Board, in their analysis "Engineering by Viewgraph," also makes distinctions among methods of presentation:

> At many points during its investigation, the Board was surprised to receive similar presentation slides [similar to the Boeing slide with all its problems] from NASA officials in place of technical reports. The Board views the endemic use of PowerPoint briefing slides instead of technical papers as an illustration of the problematic methods of technical communication at NASA.

In this question, the tool metaphor does not provide intellectual leverage. Some tools are better than others; some poor performances are the fault of the tool. Saying that the problem is with the user rather than the tool blames the victims of PP (audience, content, presenter).

Nearly all the evidence of the essay suggests that there is inherent defect in PowerPoint, unless one advances the entertaining alternative hypothesis that nearly all PP users are lightweights and nearly all users of other methods are not. This is not the case; PP has inherent defect.

I work in a large bureaucracy and everyone uses PowerPoint. I have problems with PowerPoint but how can I possibly avoid it in my talks?

Use PP only as a slide projector for a few detailed images. Provide everyone at the meeting with a substantial paper handout and talk your audience through the handout. And don't begin by saying "Today I won't be using PowerPoint." Rarely do we want to attract attention to the methodology of presentation; instead just give a nice straightforward talk accompanying the printed material.

I've seen some very good presentations using PowerPoint. What about that?

Many factors contribute to a successful presentation: most of all, excellent content clearly presented. A good speaker with good content can sometimes overcome PP's cognitive style (especially if PPPhluff, hierarchical bullet outlines, low resolution, and branding are avoided). But our evidence indicates that this rarely happens. And why should presenters have to work around the PP cognitive style? Giving a good presentation is difficult enough; we shouldn't have to fight all the time with PowerPoint also.

Your essay is very critical and about what not to do. What about ways to give a good presentation?

Well, I can recommend 3 books on how to present visual evidence! Lurking in this essay are in fact a good many practical ideas on how to give PowerPoint-free presentations. Specific advice on making public presentations is found in the third chapter of *Visual Explanations* and in the forum at www.edwardtufte.com.

Are there any other slides worthy of the Gettysburg Address parody? Seen any really good bad slides lately?

It will be difficult ever to outdo the bar chart showing minus 87 years (four score and seven years ago) in Gettysburg by Peter Norvig. But connoisseurs of the graphically preposterous have been deeply moved by a recent PP slide presented by a high-level government official to a high-level advisory council. This is a real graphic, not a parody. It invites farcical speculation that the proposed research seeks to distinguish between the Ptolemaic and Copernican hypotheses. After all, the Earth is shown at the center of the universe.

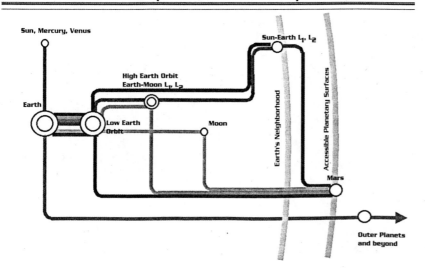

"NASA's Strategy for Human and Robotic Exploration," slide 11, Gary L. Martin, NASA Space Architect, June 10, 2003, presented to the NASA Advisory Council.